J·R

Jesus and the starving crowd

by Diane Walker

Seth was tired out! Surely it was time for lunch? He stood up straight and stretched his aching back. He looked at all the stones he had already carried to the side of the field. There were hundreds! But when he looked back at the field, there were still stones scattered all over it.

"Dad!" he shouted. "Can we stop? I'm starving!"

Ben, his father, turned round to look at him. "Yes, we've done quite well," he agreed. "We should finish clearing the stones from the field soon, so that I can dig it properly. Then you can help me plant it after school tomorrow. I thought cucumbers and onions would grow well here."

Seth sighed. That meant more hard work tomorrow! Today already seemed endless. First, he had been up at dawn to help his mother roll up the beds and pack the lunches. Then he had worked hard at synagogue school for two hours. After that, he had run up to the field to join his father.

But now, at last, it was lunch time.

"Fetch the lunches!" his father called.

Seth, his tiredness forgotten, hurried over to the oldest olive tree, where the lunches lay in the shade. He knew that his favourite lunch was waiting for him, because he'd helped his mother to pack it that morning.

Seth and Ben headed for their favourite spot at the top of the hill. From here, they could see right over the lake. Cool breezes from the water blew against their faces. It was very peaceful here, and they often dozed quietly for a few minutes after they had eaten.

But today was different.

"What's that noise?" his father said as soon as they had sat down.

Seth stopped unpacking his own bread and fishes and his father's olives and cheese so that he could listen. They could hear voices – many voices. They both stood up to see what was happening.

"Look!" his father said, pointing. There, below them, they could see crowds of people, walking along the lake shore. "Now, where could they all be going?" he wondered.

"There's a boat, too," Seth said, pointing at a fishing boat which had just drawn up on the shore.

His father shaded his eyes.

"I think it's Jesus and his friends. That's Peter's boat anyway," he told his son. "They often come over here, to be quiet and alone, I think. You know what it's like for him now. There are always so many people who want to see him and listen to him."

"They're not going to be quiet and alone today," Seth laughed, "not with all these people round them!" He sat down again. "What he says must be good and exciting if all these people have left their work just to listen to him."

His father looked down at his son. "You've never heard him, have you Seth? Why don't you take your lunch down there and listen for a bit? I'll carry on here."

Seth looked up. "Do you mind? It doesn't seem fair to leave you with all the work."

"You can make up for it tomorrow by working twice as hard!" his father said. "Off you go!"

Seth quickly bundled his food back into the basket, and set off down the hill. By the time he reached the bottom, even more people had arrived.

"I don't think I've ever seen so many people together at one time!" he thought.

Jesus was already talking, sitting high on the hill so that everyone could see and hear him. Seth struggled through to the back of the crowd to reach the water's edge. There was a rock here on which he and his father sat when they were fishing. They called it their Fishing Rock.

"I'll listen for a bit and then eat my lunch," he thought.

But Seth was soon so interested in what Jesus was saying that he forgot about his lunch. He forgot all about being hungry. He and the crowd listened as Jesus talked about God and about God's love for them. Some of the things Jesus said were hard to understand, but often he would tell stories to show what he meant. Seth began to understand why so many people said that Jesus was a good teacher.

Seth had noticed that the disciples, Jesus' friends, had been muttering together for some time. Now they went up to talk to him, and Seth stood up to stretch. He looked round in astonishment. It would soon be getting dark! He had been listening for hours! He wondered whether his father would be angry. Just as he thought this, he saw his father walking through the shallow water to join him.

"I thought you might be on our Fishing Rock!" he said. "I've already told your mother we'll be late." And he sat down next to Seth on the rock, waiting for Jesus to start talking once more.

But instead, some of Jesus' friends began to walk through the crowds, stopping now and then to ask,

"Has anyone got any food?"

"What's going on?" Seth asked his father. "Why do they want to know that?"

His father was puzzled too. "I'm sure everyone's hungry," he said. "It is getting late – time for everyone's meal. But surely they don't think anyone's got enough food for everyone to share? There's thousands of people here. All the villages round here must be empty!"

Seth laughed. "We'd need boats and carts to carry the food in – unless of course, they all want to share my lunch!" he joked. "I was so interested in what Jesus was saying that I forgot to eat it."

"It must have been exciting to make you forget food," his father replied.

One of Jesus' friends had reached them now, asking for food.

Seth held up his basket. "There's some food here," he told him, "but not much – just five bread rolls and two small fish."

"Bring it to Jesus," the disciple said, so Seth followed him through the crowd. He didn't see what good his bit of food would do. Now that he'd thought about food, he was starving again! He supposed that everyone else was, too.

They reached Jesus, and joined the other disciples there.

"Well, you were all worried about the people being hungry," Jesus said to them. "Have you managed to find any food?"

They shook their heads. One of them muttered something about how much it would cost to feed all these people.

The disciple with Seth then showed Jesus the picnic lunch. Jesus bent down and took the food from Seth.

"Thank you," he said.

Then he told his disciples to ask everyone to sit down in groups. The people moved away from the rocks, and settled on the grass.

Jesus took Seth's bread and held it up where everyone could see it.

"Thank you, Father God, for this good bread," he prayed.

Jesus asked all his disciples to line up in front of him. He filled the arms of each with bread – but where the bread came from, Seth couldn't tell. The only bread Jesus had touched was the bread Seth gave him.

Seth watched as disciple after disciple went away with their load of bread, and gave it to the people waiting around them.

Then Jesus took the fishes from Seth's basket, and held them up. "Thank you, Father God, for this good fish," he prayed.

Once more, the disciples queued up and once again they took the food round the groups of people. All of the crowd ate as much bread and fish as they wanted.

Seth stood and watched as he ate his own share of the food.

"Had enough, Seth?" Jesus asked him, smiling, and he nodded.

Jesus turned to the disciples. "Tell the people it's time for them to go home now," he said. "Then fetch some fishbaskets from the shore, and collect the scraps of food left on the ground."

Slowly, the people stood up, thanked Jesus, and said goodbye to him and to their friends. As the sky grew dark and the setting sun shone golden on the water, everyone set off for home. Seth's father came to join him.

"Was all of that your food?" he asked Seth quietly.

Seth whispered, "My food was the only food Jesus had, Dad. But there was more than that somehow. The food just kept coming and coming. Everyone had enough! And look at the baskets over there!"

Standing ready to be carried down into the village were the baskets the disciples had fetched. They were all full of bread. "I don't understand," Seth said.

"Neither do I," his father agreed, "but we both saw it happen! Let's go and tell your mother."

Together, they walked back up the hill, through the field and the old olive trees, and back to their home. The aroma of their evening meal drifted out of the doorway.

"Dad," Seth said as they went inside, "I don't think I can eat any more food tonight."

"No," his father replied, "I don't think I can! We'll have to eat it tomorrow instead!"